It Is To

Daniel J

Illustrated by Ronald Lipking

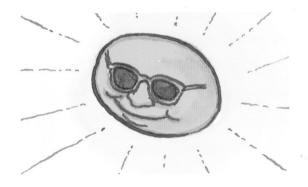

Rigby®

A Harcourt Achieve Imprint

www.Rigby.com
1-800-531-5015

"It is too hot to ride,"
said Elephant.

3

"It is too hot to play," said Elephant.

5

"It is too hot to swing," said Elephant.

"It is too hot to hop,"
said Elephant.

9

"It is too hot to walk," said Elephant.

"It is too hot to climb," said Elephant.

"It is too hot to slide," said Elephant.

"It is **not** too hot to swim!" said Elephant.